ARIAKE

Ariake

poems of love and longing

by the women courtiers
of ancient Japan

Illustrations by Rae Grant

Foreword by Liza Dalby

CHRONICLE BOOKS

SAN FRANCISCO

Pp. 13, 23, 52, 53, 59, 60, 62, Reprinted from *An Introduction to Japanese Court Poetry*, by Earl Miner, with translations by the author and Robert H. Brower with the permission of the publishers, Stanford University Press. © 1968 by the Board of the Trustees of the Leland Stanford Junior University.

Pp.16, 17, 27, 29, 31, 32, 36, 37, 44, 45, 47, 48, 49, 68, 75, 76, Reprinted from *Kokin Wakashu: The First Imperial Anthology of Japanese Poetry*, translated and annotated by Helen Craig McCullough with the permission of the publishers, Stanford University Press. © 1985 by the Board of the Trustees of the Leland Stanford Junior University.

Pp. 10, 14, 19, 20, 24, 28, 35, 38, 41, 42, 50, 54, 57, 58, 63, 64, 67, 69, 70, 73, 74, 79, Reprinted from *A Waka Anthology: Volume One: The Gem Glistening Cup*, translated, with a commentary and notes, by Edwin A. Cranston with the permission of the publishers, Stanford University Press. © 1993 by the Board of the Trustees of the Leland Stanford Junior University.

Edited, illustrated, and designed by Rae Grant Design, New York City.

Printed in China

Library of Congress Cataloging-in Publication Data available.

ISBN 0-8118-2813-1

Distributed in Canada by
Raincoast Books
8680 Cambie Street
Vancouver, BC V6P 6M9

10 9 8 7 6 5 4 3 2 1

Chronicle Books
85 Second Street
San Francisco, CA 94105

www.chroniclebooks.com

For Perry, Gwendolyn,
and for my mother, Doris

Foreword

Ariake, or "the waning moon at dawn," was an image associated foremost with love in the ancient courts of Japan. Two lovers, absorbed in their passion, knew that when the dawn moon floated toward the western hills, they would soon have to part. The man might fumble in the dim light, looking for his fan; the lady might straighten his robes and smooth his hair. In the sky, the pale moon hovered before disappearing over the horizon. The lady would return to her room to await the poem she knew he would send, artfully folded, secured with a flowering twig. When it came, she lingered over each word, choosing related images to weave into her own reply.

Few societies integrated poetry into daily life as devotedly as the court of Japan's Heian era (A.D. 794–1192). Poetry commemorated social events from births to funerals, and honored the most intensely private moments. Spring picnics inspired paeans to nature. Courtly poetry matches featured designated themes, and teams of courtiers vied for imperial favor with clever turns of phrase and evocative imagery. Folding screens, which customarily adorned both court and home, displayed lyrical pairings of poems and paintings. And, of course, poetry was the language, par excellence, of love. Courtly love affairs blossomed, took root, and withered—all punctuated by exchanges of verse.

The most renowned poets of the era were women. Not the passive objects of desire characteristic of Western courtly love, these women were passionate and demonstrative, writing poetry about their lovers and themselves in brief, intense outbursts of image and rhythm. The ninth-century lady, Ono no Komachi, legendary for her wit and beauty, runs along the path of dreams every night to meet her lover—yet the vision she pursues in endless dreams pales next to the briefest glimpse of him in waking life. An anonymous poet fusses with her pillow—how was it arranged that night she dreamed of him? Can she make him come to her again? The maiden, Ato no Tobira, having seen a man once by moonlight is now visited by him in dreams. Dream or reality? How love confounds the senses.

In affairs of the heart, etiquette demanded a morning-after poem, and while their impetus may have been spontaneous, the poems were most carefully crafted. Quite early in its history, the poetry of the Japanese court coalesced into one particular format—the 31-syllable waka. The waka consists of a patterned sequence of 5 syllables, followed by a line of 7, then 5 again; a pause in the phrasing; then two lines of 7 each. This kind of poetry was not necessarily an expression of individual genius (although, of course, some people were much better at it than others) so much as it was a form of highly aestheticized communication. For an educated courtier, composing a waka was almost as natural as speaking. The Japanese language falls easily into the waka patterns.

By the eighth century, Japan had borrowed from neighboring China a system of graphic symbols. From this, the Japanese created their own writing symbols, enabling them to preserve their poetry on paper. It is not surprising that the content of Japanese poetry was also influenced by Chinese canons of poetic taste. Images like languishing ladies in autumn or elegant confusions like plum blossoms mistaken for snow were originally Chinese conceits. But the Japanese formed their own notions of what made poetry poetic, and this is most evident in their intensely personal poems of love and longing.

Japanese poetry has traditionally conformed to set topics, of which the categories of the seasons make up the greatest number. But it is the poetry about love that strikes the modern reader as most memorable. Of all human experiences, love bends the themes of the seasons and of nature to its demands.

Ultimately, these love poems enjoyed a much wider audience than the two lovers alone. The Japanese cultivated a place for this essentially private poetry in the public literary domain. As a result we can, to this day, be privy to the most intimate desires of the ancient Japanese courtiers. Despite the passage of time and the distortion of translation, the poems retain an astonishing immediacy. Each verse crystallizes the emotion which inspired the words so many years ago. This exquisite collection brings together some of the best surviving love poems, recalling an age when the sentiments were fresh, the longing was palpable, and the language was that of love.

Love fulfilled is its own reward. Love frustrated is restless and seeks expression. Its salvation is poetry.

Liza Dalby

As the thread of my breath

This held longing: reeling pain;

Let the jewel-thread snap,

The wild scattering begin—

And if the world knows, it knows.

Anonymous

Guide me on my way—

My boat rows on across a sea

Of trackless waves,

And I cannot tell where I am bound—

O wind that blows up on all sides!

Princess Shokushi

The white drops of dew

That glisten in the evening sun

There in my garden

Fade no more quickly from the grass

Than I faint from my desire.

Lady Kasa

All too soon, I fear,

Wild sobs will expose my love,

As wind-driven waves,

Crashing onto the beaches,

Lay bare the roots of the pines.

Anonymous

If I might offer

To give my life in exchange

To one who would bear

The burden of this passion,

Ah, how easy death would be!

Anonymous

9

I shall think of you;

You too do not forget me:

Like the wind that sweeps

Ceaselessly across the bay,

Let us never cease our love.

Lady Kasa

Don't you cut the brush

Growing on the riverbank

High above Saho River;

Leave it as it is,

So when springtime comes around

We'll have a place to hide.

Lady Ōtomo of Sakanoue

Brought by the breeze,

The scent of flowers in my sleeve

Is what awakes me

On a pillow richly fragrant

With the brief spring night of dreams.

Shunzei's Daughter

Hidden-in-winter

The spring moors are all aflame—

And he who burns them,

Can he never burn enough,

That he now sets fire to my heart?

Anonymous

Pillows know, they say,

And so we slept without one.

Why then do rumors

Like swirling pillars of dust

Rise as high as the heavens?

Lady Ise

Being helpless

In my desire for him,

I came out,

Unaware of the spring rain

That was falling even then.

Anonymous

While I asked myself

Whether you might be coming

Or I might go there,

The hesitant moon appeared,

And I slept, the door unlocked.

Anonymous

How far from enough

Seemed that brief meeting with you

Lighted by the moon

As it voyaged through the skies

In the deep heart of the night!

Anonymous

Because of this love,

My body has been transformed

Into a shadow,

But not, alas, the shadow

That follows your every step.

Anonymous

As one hears the cry

Of a crane in the darkness

Far off at night,

Must I hear but rumors of you,

With never a chance to meet?

Lady Kasa

More than the color

It is the fragrance I find

A source of delight.

Whose sleeve might have brushed against

The plum tree beside my house?

Anonymous

We cannot tell now,

But let us try a small test:

If we both survive,

Will it be I who forget

Or you who fail to visit?

Anonymous

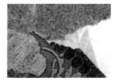

Here in my garden

All in flower is the plum,

And the moon is fine—

Night by night I wait for you,

You only, to show them.

Anonymous

So it is because

My true love so yearns for me,

That he comes in dreams

In the night as black as beads—

And for me there is no sleep.

Anonymous

In the blackberry

Night I saw you one last time,

But I let you go

Without meeting you at dawn,

And now I have learned regret.

Otogami

Whatever the cost,

I must keep him from leaving.

Scatter, you cherry blossoms,

Until he can no longer

Know which is the way to go.

Anonymous

As night succeeds night,

I seek in vain to decide

Where my pillow should go.

How did I sleep on the night

When you appeared in my dream?

Anonymous

8

Lov

The words "I love you,"

Issuing from lips as leaves

Sprout from trees and shrubs,

Alone will keep their color,

Unaltered as autumns pass.

Anonymous

Am I to go on,

Forever yearning, my thoughts

Tangled as seaweed

Swaying with the waves, neither

Drifting out nor coming in?

Anonymous

When longing for you

Torments me beyond my strength,

I reverse my robe,

Raiment of seed-black night,

And put it on inside out.

Ono no Komachi

Were you a string of beads

I would wind you about my arm,

But since you are a man

Of the actual, mortal world,

You are hard in the winding.

The Elder Maiden of the Ōtomo of Sakanoue

Now that the fragrance

Rises from the orange trees

That wait till June to bloom,

I am reminded of those scented sleeves

And wonder about that person of my past.

Anonymous

O cord of life! ·

Threading through the jewel of my soul,

If you break, break now:

My strength will go if this continues,

Unable to bear such a fearful strain.

Princess Shokushi

When we could have met

Any time, any night,

Why did we do it—

Why did we choose that night to meet,

And all this thicket of talk?

The Elder Maiden of the Ōtomo of Sakanoue

てんとり
上るの
ろてんとをさん
とん
いとく
そく
こくとり
とりと
リとり

Where the plovers cry

On the lip of Saho River

The shallows are broad—

I'll lay a plank bridge for you,

For I'm sure that you will come.

Lady Ōtomo of Sakanoue

If it is but sleep,

Why, I can sleep with anyone;

But it is you, my love,

Who drifted with me like the seaweed

Of the offing, for whose word I wait.

Anonymous

Lying down alone,

I am so confused in yearning for you

That I have forgot

The tangles of my long black hair,

Desiring the one who stroked it clear.

Izumi Shikibu

My mind is dazzled—

Did you come to visit me?

Or I to you?

Was our night a dream? Reality?

Was I sleeping? Or was I awake?

Shrine Priestess of Ise

Although my feet

Never cease running to you

On the path of dreams,

Such nights of love are never worth

One glimpse of you in reality.

Ono no Komachi

Have I let my love

Slip out where the world may know?

I had a dream

Where I saw my box of combs—

And I was opening it!

Lady Kasa

Hidden in the clouds,

Where it goes we cannot say,

But I yearn for it—

The moon, my love, are you eager

To gaze on it as I?

The Maiden Ōyake

[127]

Only one fleeting

Glance by the light of the moon,

The sky-traveler,

Had that man and I, and yet

Now I see him in my dreams.

The Maiden Ato no Tobira

You intend, it seems,

To make me die of this love,

For all through the night,

Black as leopard-flower seeds,

You come to visit my dreams.

Anonymous

Till the rough-gem moon

Stood renewed in the sky

You did not come—

I have seen you in my dreams,

Longing for you all the while.

Lady Ōtomo of Sakanoue

Though in my heart

I have longed for you, never

Forgetting for a day,

You are a man over whom

Talk grows like a jungle.

Lady Ōtomo of Sakanoue

After spring has come

The shrike goes plunging in the reeds

And cannot be seen—

But I will spy it out, my love,

The place where you have your home.

Anonymous

Do not look at me

Tenderly as tender-grass

In a fence of reeds—

If you smile at me like that

People are sure to know.

Anonymous

Just because of you,

Stories about me have spread

As a springtime haze

Envelops blossoming flowers

On fields and mountains alike.

Anonymous

Were I to send word,

"The moon is fine, and the night

Is also pleasant,"

It would be like saying, "Come."

It is not that I do not wait.

Anonymous

Look at this keepsake

And remember me, my love;

All the gem-bright year,

Long as its thread of shining days,

I too shall think of you.

Lady Kasa